K-1 Fiance Visa for Vietnam

How to Organize Documents for Consulate Interview

T Nguyen

K-1 Fiance Visa for Vietnam is intended to help couples organize documents for their K-1 Visa case in Vietnam. It is important for applicants to organize documents themselves, so they will be more familiar with the documents. Applicants should be able to quickly present the documents to the consulate officers during the interview. The interview itself might last only 20 minutes, so the Vietnamese fiancé being interviewed should not spend precious time searching through documents during the interview. Knowing where all documents are and presenting them in an organized way will help increase confidence during the interview.

Outlines and templates are provided to help organize the documents. This book is intended as one resource to help with the K-1 visa process. K-1 applicants should also consider seeking information and advice from free sources available on the internet, as well as from immigration lawyers and "dich vu" document preparers.

This book is organized to look like a case file. The case is a situation where the man meets the woman (or the woman meets the man) face-to-face in Vietnam on the first trip. He takes a second trip to Vietnam for the Dam Hoi engagement party. Then he takes a third trip to Vietnam after the engagement party. Some people take more or fewer trips to Vietnam. If this is the situation, the documents and photos should be labeled and organized to specify which trip the documents and photos apply to. For example, label the Trip # on the documents, Trip #1, Trip #2, Trip #3, and so forth. This book only outlines a case for three trips, so be sure to change the outline if more or fewer trips were taken.

Most of the documents organized in this book are the optional documents given to USCIS and the consulate in Vietnam. Many of the required documents are government forms, such as the application, affidavit of support, birth certificate, Ho Khau, etc. and English translations of some of those documents. These documents can be easily identified and do not need to be labeled in ways similar to documents in this book. The optional documents, however, must be labeled and organized for the consulate official. These document provide proof that the relationship exists and is true and bona fide, with marriage in the United States as the eventual goal.

The outlines at the beginning of the book suggest some of the optional documents that can be submitted. If there are other documents not listed that can support the case, try to label and organize them in a way consistent with the optional documents shown. Some documents proving that the couple have met face-to-face and are engaged should have been sent to USCIS with the initial K1 visa application. Therefore, the consulate officers will already have viewed those documents by the time of the interview. Therefore, while the consulate requests that the applicant bring **Before Engagement** and **After Engagement** documents to the interview, the consulate officer might focus on the more recent **After Engagement** documents brought to the interview.

The goal is to create a good portfolio of documents and photos to present to the Consulate. The portfolio should include documents from each trip to Vietnam, documents relating to the Dam Hoi Engagement, and many photos taken together and taken together with family and friends. Once the portfolio is gathered, it is important to organize the documents and photos into a case file that will be easily understood by anyone, especially the consulate officer.

Remember that this book offers just one suggestion for organizing the optional documents. There are many ways to label and organize the documents.

Outline Key

Words that are in capital letters in the outline should be changed in the following way:

DATE : Enter the date for which the event took place.

DATE – DATE : Enter the beginning and ending dates for the event.

CITY : Enter the city for each leg of trip, starting with CITY #1, the start of trip.

MONTH YEAR : Enter the month in words. Enter the year in 4-digit format.

FIANCE NAME : Enter fiance's name.

Documents to Gather Prior to K-1 Application

Submit proof that the couple met recently, that there is a bona fide relationship, and that the couple has been engaged. Consider submitting at least some of the following documents:

Vietnam Trip #1 – Before Engagement
    Receipt
    Itinerary
    Airline Ticket
    Boarding Passes (each leg of trip)
    Arrival-Departure Declaration
    Visa

Phone Records – Before Engagement

Mail Records – Before Engagement
    Copies of Letters or Greeting Cards, with mailing envelopes (showing correspondence with each other)

Email Records
    Copies of Emails – Before Engagement

Vietnam Trip #2 - Engagement
    Receipt
    Itinerary
    Airline Ticket
    Boarding Passes (each leg of trip)
    Arrival-Departure Declaration
    Visa

Dam Hoi Engagement Documents
    Receipts – Engagement Party
    Receipt – Engagement Ring

Photos (with and without family and friends)
    Photos – Before Engagement
    Photos – Dam Hoi Engagement Party

Documents to Gather during Entire Process

Vietnam Trip #1 – Before Engagement
- Receipt
- Itinerary
- Airline Ticket
- Boarding Passes (each leg of trip)
- Arrival-Departure Declaration
- Visa

Vietnam Trip #2 - Engagement
- Receipt
- Itinerary
- Airline Ticket
- Boarding Passes (each leg of trip)
- Arrival-Departure Declaration
- Visa

Vietnam Trip #3 – After Engagement
- Receipt
- Itinerary
- Airline Ticket
- Boarding Passes (each leg of trip)
- Arrival-Departure Declaration
- Visa

Phone Records
    Before Engagement
    After Engagement

Mail Records - Before and After Engagement
    Copies of Letters or Greeting Cards, with
    mailing envelopes (showing
    correspondence with each other)

Chat Records
    Chat Log – Before Engagement
    Chat Transcript – Before Engagement
    (1 sample)
    Chat Log – After Engagement
    Chat Transcript – After Engagement
    (1 sample)

Email Records
    Copies of Emails – Before Engagement
    Copies of Emails – After Engagement

Dam Hoi Engagement Documents
    Receipts – Engagement Party
    Receipt – Engagement Ring

Wedding Preparation Documents
    Wedding Plans: church, civil, etc…
    Reception Plans
    Letters confirming plans

Other Documents
    Receipts – English language school
    Receipts – Money transfers

Photos (with and without family and friends)
    Photos – Before Engagement
    Photos – Dam Hoi Engagement Party
    Photos – After Engagement

Documents to Present during Interview at Consulate

Consulate requests that documents and photos are organized and divided into two categories: Before Engagement and After Engagement. Organize the documents in the following manner prior to interview:

Documents – Before Engagement

Vietnam Trip #1 – Before Engagement
    Receipt
    Itinerary
    Airline Ticket
    Boarding Passes (each leg of trip)
    Arrival-Departure Declaration
    Visa

Phone Records – Before Engagement
Mail Records – Before Engagement
Chat Log – Before Engagement
Chat Transcript – Before Engagement (1 sample)
Copies of Emails – Before Engagement

Documents – Engagement

Vietnam Trip #2 - Engagement
    Receipt
    Itinerary
    Airline Ticket
    Boarding Passes (each leg of trip)
    Arrival-Departure Declaration
    Visa

Receipts – Engagement Party
Receipt – Engagement Ring

Documents – After Engagement

Vietnam Trip #3 – After Engagement
    Receipt
    Itinerary
    Airline Ticket
    Boarding Passes (each leg of trip)
    Arrival-Departure Declaration
    Visa

Phone Records – After Engagement
Mail Records – After Engagement
Chat Log – After Engagement
Chat Transcript – After Engagement (1 sample)
Copies of Emails – After Engagement

Letters confirming wedding and/or reception plans
Receipts – English language school
Receipts – Money transfers

Photos

Photos – Before Engagement
Photos – Engagement Party
Photos – After Engagement

Before Engagement

Airline Ticket Receipt: Vietnam Trip # 1
(DATE   -   DATE   )

Itinerary: Vietnam Trip # 1
(DATE   -   DATE   )

Airline Ticket: Vietnam Trip # 1
(DATE - DATE)

Boarding Passes: Vietnam Trip # 1
(DATE   -   DATE   )
CITY #1 to CITY #2 to CITY #3…

<u>Arrival-Departure Declaration:</u>
Vietnam Trip # 1
(DATE   -   DATE   )

<u>Vietnam Visa</u>: Vietnam Trip # 1
(DATE   -   DATE   )

Phone Bills: Before Engagement
(MONTH YEAR – MONTH YEAR)

<u>Copies of Letters</u>: Before Engagement

(Make copies of letters and greeting cards and copies of the envelopes used to send the cards. This shows the dates the mail were sent. Can copy letters and greeting cards on one side of paper and envelope on reverse side for better organization. Attach a coversheet like this one to the front.)

Chat Log: Before Engagement
(MONTH YEAR – MONTH YEAR)

Sample Chat Transcript: Before Engagement
(DATE)

<u>Emails</u>: Before Engagement

(Combine emails by each month first by fastening them together. Then use a large paperclip to join all the Before Engagement Emails together. Attach a coversheet like this one to the front.)

Emails: Before Engagement
(MONTH YEAR)

Emails: Before Engagement
(MONTH YEAR)

Emails: Before Engagement
(MONTH YEAR)

Engagement

Airline Ticket Receipt: Vietnam Trip # 2
(DATE   -   DATE   )

Itinerary: Vietnam Trip # 2
(DATE   -   DATE   )

Airline Ticket: Vietnam Trip # 2
(DATE   -   DATE   )

Boarding Passes: Vietnam Trip # 2
(DATE   -   DATE   )
CITY #1 to CITY #2 to CITY #3…

Arrival-Departure Declaration:
Vietnam Trip # 2
(DATE   -   DATE   )

Vietnam Visa: Vietnam Trip # 2
(DATE   -   DATE   )

<u>Receipts</u>: Dam Hoi Engagement Party
(DATE)

Receipt: Engagement Ring

After Engagement

Airline Ticket Receipt: Vietnam Trip # 3
(DATE   -   DATE   )

Itinerary: Vietnam Trip # 3
(DATE   -   DATE   )

Airline Ticket: Vietnam Trip # 3
(DATE   -   DATE   )

Boarding Passes: Vietnam Trip # 3
(DATE   -   DATE   )
CITY #1 to CITY #2 to CITY #3…

Arrival-Departure Declaration:
Vietnam Trip # 3
(DATE - DATE)

Vietnam Visa: Vietnam Trip # 3
(DATE   -   DATE   )

Phone Bills: After Engagement
(MONTH YEAR – MONTH YEAR)

<u>Copies of Letters</u>: After Engagement

(Make copies of letters and greeting cards and copies of the envelopes used to send the cards. This shows the dates the mail were sent. Can copy letters and greeting cards on one side of paper and envelope on reverse side for better organization. Attach a coversheet like this one to the front.)

Chat Log: After Engagement
(MONTH YEAR – MONTH YEAR)

Sample Chat Transcript: After Engagement
(DATE)

Emails: **After Engagement**
(MONTH YEAR – MONTH YEAR)

(Combine emails by each month first by fastening them together. Then use a large paperclip to join all the After Engagement Emails together. Attach a coversheet like this one to the front.)

Emails: After Engagement
(MONTH YEAR)

Emails: After Engagement
(MONTH YEAR)

Emails: After Engagement
(MONTH YEAR)

Letter from Church
(confirming wedding plans)

Letter or Receipt
(confirming reception plans)

Receipts: Money Transfers to FIANCE NAME

Receipts: English Language Classes for FIANCE NAME

Photo Organization

Build a good photo portfolio by including many photos taken together as a couple and also taken together with family and friends. Be sure to include many photos of the Engagement Party because that party is very important in Vietnamese culture. On back of each photo, write **Vietnam Trip #1**, **Vietnam Trip #2**, **Vietnam Trip #3**, or **Engagement Party** and provide the location and date.

Put the photos from each category into separate, strong Ziploc bags, labeled in the way below.

<u>Photos</u>: Before Engagement
<u>Photos</u>: Dam Hoi Engagement Party
<u>Photos</u>: After Engagement

The photos should be given to the consulate officer during the interview. This is done by passing the photos under the glass window. Most likely, the photos will be returned during the interview.

Document Organization

For original documents smaller than letter-size paper, tape the documents to letter-size paper. Write labels at the top of each sheet. For copies of documents, write labels at the top of each paper. Try to be consistent with size of paper for less aggravation and better presentation. Consider printing forms on letter-size paper (8.5 x 11 inches) if possible. Also consider trimming copies on large-size sheets to letter-size sheets if possible. Be careful not to cut any original important documents, like government issued documents and forms, birth certificates, etc.

Staple, paperclip, or use Acco fasteners to combine similar documents, depending on the thickness of the combined documents. For example, staple each phone bill that is more than one page. Then paperclip or fasten all phone bills together. Likewise, separate all emails by month. Then hole-punch and use Acco fasteners to join them together because the email records tend to be very thick.

Use folders and binders to organize the documents in the way shown below. Carry the folders and binders in a backpack to keep everything together.

1. One Folder with required documents

This folder contains the required documents specified in the letter from the consulate. Keep these documents separate from the optional documents to present to the consulate officer at the interview. The required documents will need to be given to consulate staff prior to the actual interview.

Left side of folder – Make copies of all required documents and label everything. These copies are for your own future reference. The consulate will not keep the copies.

Right side of folder – Keep original documents on one side. For small, single items like ID card and receipt of payment to consulate: Tape to letter-size paper to keep the items better organized and to keep them from getting lost.

2. One Thick File Folder with copies of optional documents

This folder should have four sections and must be large enough to hold all optional documents, especially the thick email and chat documents. Make sure the two types of documents are clearly separated: Put **Before Engagement** documents toward the front, **Engagement** documents in the middle, and **After Engagement** documents toward the back. Put the Ziploc bags containing the photos in the fourth section. This folder is the most important folder during the actual interview. Be ready to give the consulate officials these documents and photos by passing them under the glass window during the actual interview. Consulate officials might keep some of these documents. Be prepared to answer any questions about the documents and photos.

3. One Zipper Binder with originals for the optional documents

This folder contains the originals for the documents from which copies in the thick file folder were made. Separate **Before Engagement, Engagement,** and **After Engagement** documents. Consulate officials might request to see these original documents during the interview. More likely they will not request the documents, so the binder probably will not have to be opened. But bring those documents, just in case.

Good Luck with the interview.

www.ingramcontent.com/pod-product-compliance
Lightning Source LLC
Chambersburg PA
CBHW081355280526
45788CB00009B/2891